Spiritual Survival: How Faith and Preparedness Go Hand in Hand in a Chaotic World

A Christian's Guide to Embracing

Faith and Practical Prepping

Peter Thompson

Copyright © 2024 by Peter Thompson

Book Cover by Peter Thompson

Illustrations by Peter Thompson

1st edition 2024

ARMOR OF GOD

HELMET OF SALVATION
BREASTPLATE OF RIGHTEOUSNESS
BELT OF TRUTH
SHIELD OF FAITH
SWORD OF THE SPIRIT
SHOES OF THE GOSPEL OF PEACE

Preface

What does it take to truly be ready for the unknown? It starts with faith and ends with action.

In "Spiritual Survival: How Faith and Preparedness Go Hand in Hand in a Chaotic World," you'll find an empowering guide that combines spiritual wisdom with practical preparedness. Learn to navigate life's challenges by:

- Strengthening your **faith** and relying on God's promises.

- Developing key **survival skills** that will help you thrive in any situation.

- Crafting a customized preparedness plan that reflects your **Christian values**.

- Building a resilient **mindset** that conquers fear and embraces hope.

- Connecting with a **community** of like-minded believers who share your commitment to faith and readiness.

Packed with inspiration, biblical insights, and real-life examples, this book will transform the way you approach preparedness. It's not about surviving—it's about thriving with confidence, courage, and clarity, no matter what the world throws your way.

Get ready to face the future with faith and purpose. Your journey starts now!

Acknowledgments

I would like to express my deepest gratitude to my family and friends for their unwavering support and encouragement throughout this journey.

I am profoundly grateful to my mother for her invaluable insights, feedback, and inspiration. Your exceptional contributions have been instrumental in bringing this project to life.

To my amazing wife, thank you for believing in all my crazy ideas and supporting all my adventures. You fill our home with love and laughter. Your dedication to our family is unmatched.

I want to thank God for the strength, guidance, and inspiration provided during the writing of this book. My hope is that these words will help others find faith, hope, and courage in their own lives.

To my readers, thank you for your curiosity, passion, and willingness to explore the intersection of faith and preparedness. It is for you that this book was written, and I hope it brings you insight, comfort, and encouragement.

Table of Contents

Contents

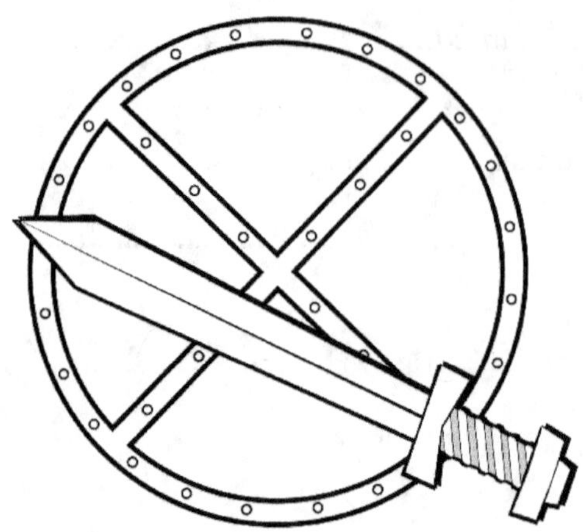

Introduction

What do you prepare for when you have no idea what's coming next? And what if everything you thought about preparedness missed the most critical aspect?

It's enough to make anyone feel unprepared, but what if true preparedness is more than stockpiling supplies or learning the latest in survival skills? What if it were also about equipping your heart and mind for the battles unseen: those that shake your confidence, test your faith, and challenge your inner peace?

If you're like me, 2020 was a wake-up call that rattled everything I thought I knew about preparedness. I realized that no amount of stockpiled food or supplies could truly prepare me for the fear, uncertainty, and doubt creeping into my heart.

That's the year when I learned one of life's greatest lessons—not real preparedness with a full pantry but—how to strengthen your heart and mind. It's preparedness for storms you can't see coming, battles you can't fight with your hands, and crises that interrogate not just your body but your very soul.

That's when I first stumbled upon the concept of spiritual preparedness—not the kind that braces you for physical survival, but the kind that equips you to weather the storms internally. When we are taking stock of our preps, spiritual preparedness needs to be at the top of that checklist. Now, at the very core of spiritual preparedness, an idea so powerful is relayed in words through the Bible: the armor of God. Found in Ephesians 6:10-18, this isn't just a spiritual metaphor—it is a foundation for living a balanced life of faith and readiness.

Finally, the Armor of God is meant to provide us with tools: truth, righteousness, peace, faith, salvation, and the Word of God. These are the sorts of things we need to stand against the most powerful challenges life can hurl at us, whether from outside ourselves or from within. This is not just defensive armor but a way to thrive, to be resilient, and to live on purpose, regardless of whatever we face.

Whether you're just starting out with emergency preparedness, or you've been doing it for years, and whether faith is a new idea for you or has always been part of your life, I invite you to explore how combining these two elements can transform your approach to life's challenges and uncertainties. Let's go on this journey together—discovering how faith and readiness are not just compatible but truly rely on each other to navigate our changing world.

Welcome to The Prayerful Prepper, where faith meets readiness in a changing world.

ARMOR OF GOD

HELMET OF SALVATION
BREASTPLATE OF RIGHTEOUSNESS
BELT OF TRUTH
SWORD OF THE SPIRIT
SHIELD OF FAITH
SHOES OF THE GOSPEL OF PEACE

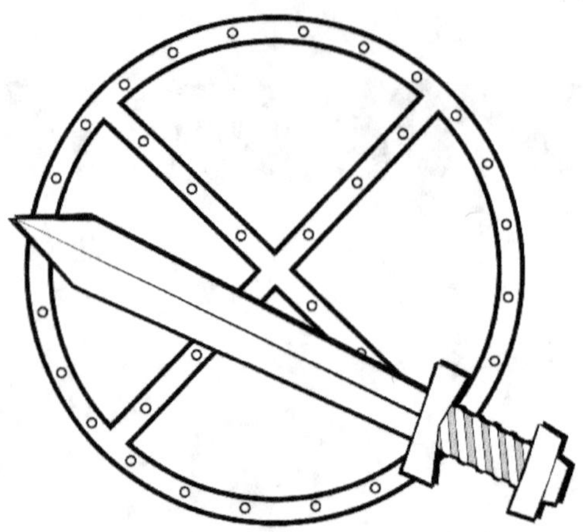

Chapter 1
Understanding the Armor of God

In any battle (or survival situation), having the right equipment is crucial, and that's just as true in our spiritual lives. The Apostle Paul understood this when he wrote about the armor of God in Ephesians 6:10-18. But what does this armor look like in today's world? How can we put it on daily and use it to stand firm against life's challenges? Should we consider this the number one prep for everyday survival?

This chapter breaks down each piece of spiritual armor and shows how it can help us become spiritually prepared for whatever may come our way. Whether you're dealing with personal struggles, societal upheaval, or natural disasters, this armor isn't just for surviving—it's for thriving.

Let's explore each piece of the Armor of God and how it relates to our daily lives, starting with the **Belt of Truth**.

Ephesians 6:10-18 (NIV)

Finally, be strong in the Lord and in his mighty power. Put on the full **armor of God**, *so that you can take your stand against the devil's schemes. For our struggle is not against flesh and blood, but against the rulers, against the authorities, against the powers of this dark world and against the spiritual forces of evil in the heavenly realms. Therefore, put on the full* **armor of God**, *so that when the day of evil comes, you may be able to stand your ground, and after you have done everything, to stand. Stand firm then, with the* **belt of truth** *buckled around your waist, with the* **breastplate of righteousness** *in place, and with your* **feet fitted with** *the readiness that comes from* **the gospel of peace**. *In addition to all this, take up the* **shield of faith**, *with which you can extinguish all the flaming arrows of the evil one. Take the* **helmet of salvation** *and the* **sword of the Spirit**, *which is the word of God. And pray in the Spirit on all occasions with all kinds of prayers and requests. With this in mind, be alert and always keep on praying for all the Lord's people.*

Belt of Truth

Alright, let's start with the **Belt of Truth**. Picture a soldier preparing for battle—the belt is the first piece of armor they put on. It's not just an accessory; it's crucial. The belt holds everything else in place and provides a foundation for the rest of the armor.

Truth is foundational. Proverbs 12:22 says, "The Lord detests lying lips, but he delights in people who are trustworthy." When we speak and live in truth, we align ourselves with God's values, and that gives us strength and stability.

I remember being a kid, maybe 7 or 8 years old, and finding a wallet stuffed with money and cards while at a lake where my family was attending a family and friends retreat with our church. At the time, to me, it seemed like a fortune, and

I was tempted to keep the cash and toss the wallet. This was the first real test of my integrity that I can recall.

Now, some might laugh at me or say I was naive, but for me, the choice was surprisingly simple. Finders keepers, right? Plus, who would know? But that Belt of Truth started feeling mighty tight! I realized that compromising on even 'small' truths can unravel our entire spiritual wardrobe.

As John Stott wisely puts it, "Truth holds everything else together. Falsehood is the great disintegrator—it breaks apart marriages, families, friendships, governments, and churches. Truth is the foundation of trust, and trust is the foundation of all human relationships." Without truth, everything else falls apart—it's like building a house on sand.

How to Wear the Belt of Truth Daily

- Start with God's Word: Make it your first source of truth each day.
- Practice Radical Honesty: Even in the little things.
- Ask Yourself: Is what I'm doing or saying aligned with God's truth?

Breastplate of Righteousness

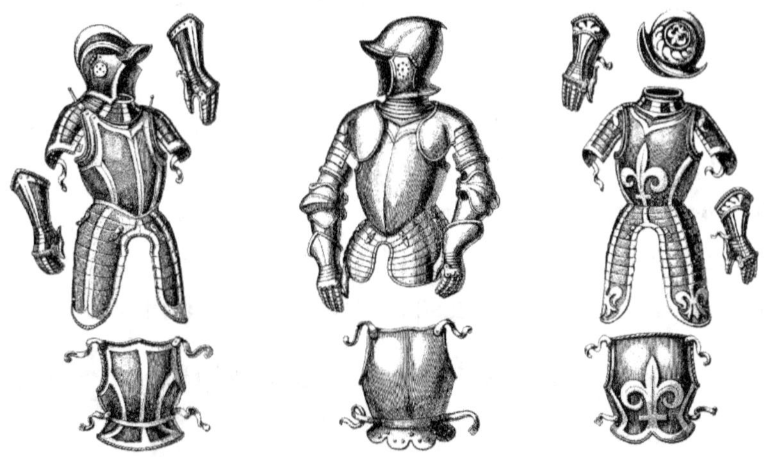

Next up, we have the **Breastplate of Righteousness**. Think about getting ready for a big game again—you put on a chest protector to guard your heart and lungs, your most vital organs. Similarly, the Breastplate of Righteousness protects your spiritual heart.

Proverbs 4:23 tells us, "Above all else, guard your heart, for everything you do flows from it." This breastplate isn't just about being perfect; it's about striving to live a life that honors God in our everyday choices.

I worked in construction in the past. It is common for contractors to cut corners to save time and money. The shortcuts would be hidden, but over time, the defects would eventually show, compromising the whole structure's integrity. I was tempted to take the easy way out too, but wearing the Breastplate of Righteousness meant choosing to do the right thing, even if it cost me more time or money. And you know what? That choice saved me from a lot of trouble later on.

John MacArthur puts it this way: "The breastplate of righteousness isn't just about the righteousness of Christ that we receive at salvation; it's about living a holy life… one that's separated from sin." It's not about being perfect but about making progress toward God's standard.

How to Wear the Breastplate of Righteousness Daily

- ➢ Pray for Guidance: Ask God to help you make righteous choices.
- ➢ Evaluate Your Decisions: Are they in line with God's principles?
- ➢ Seek Accountability: Connect with others who share your values.

Shoes of the Gospel of Peace

Now, let's lace up the **Shoes of the Gospel of Peace**. Have you ever tried running or hiking in the wrong shoes? Or danced in a pair that just didn't fit right? It's a mess—you slip, you stumble, and you don't get very far. The same goes for our spiritual lives. These shoes give us the grip we need to stand firm and the comfort to keep going, no matter what.

Ephesians 2:14 reminds us, "He himself is our peace..." That's talking about Jesus, who breaks down barriers and brings true peace. He's the one who gives us the footing to stand firm, even when everything around us is shaky.

I'll never forget when a big storm hit our area a few years ago. It knocked out the power for days, brought trees crashing down, and left everyone on edge. And this was in the middle of winter up here in the Northeast! But my mom had her spiritual shoes on—grounded in God's peace, she stayed calm and helped our neighbors. That peace spread, and it made a huge difference in a tough situation.

Charles Spurgeon said, "Rough roads grow smooth when these blessed feet are worn. And sharing that peace is an essential part of the gospel." When we walk in God's peace, it's like smoothing out the rough patches not just for ourselves, but for others too.

How to Lace Up the Shoes of Peace Daily

➢ Begin with Quiet: Let God's peace settle in before the day begins.
➢ Take a Breath: When things get chaotic, remind yourself of God's promises.
➢ Be a Peacemaker: Look for opportunities to bring peace to others.

Shield of Faith

Alright, spiritual warrior, let's talk about one of the most versatile pieces of your spiritual gear, the **Shield of Faith**. I know, I know—a shield? Sounds like something out of a medieval knight story, right? But trust me, this shield is even cooler than what you've seen in the movies.

Imagine you're in the thick of life's battlefield. Arrows of doubt are flying at you, spears of fear are coming from another side, and fiery darts of worry are raining down from above. Sound familiar? I've been there more times than I can count!

Proverbs 30:5 tells us, "Every word of God is flawless; He is a shield to those who take refuge in Him." This verse reminds us that God's Word is our ultimate protection. Martyn Lloyd-Jones, a well-known minister, explained it like this: "Faith isn't just mentally agreeing with the gospel; it's about having full confidence in Jesus and what He's done for you. It means knowing, deep down, that the Son of God loved you and gave Himself for you."

Let me share a personal story. Back in 2008, I lost my job unexpectedly—something a lot of us experienced during that time. Bills started piling up, and my savings were running low. Every day felt like a new wave of "what ifs" and "how will I ever...?" It felt like I was constantly under attack.

It was during this time that I had to learn to pick up my Shield of Faith daily. I clung to scriptures that reminded me of God's provision, like Philippians 4:19: "And my God will meet all your needs according to the riches of his glory in Christ Jesus." I made a decision to trust in His promises, even when the circumstances looked bleak. And you know what? That faith acted like a shield, blocking out the fear and helping me move forward step by step.

How to Pick Up the Shield of Faith Daily

- ➢ Know Your Shield: Get familiar with God's promises—they're what your shield is made of!
- ➢ Practice Your Stance: Start every day by re-affirming your faith, it's like a spiritual workout.
- ➢ Keep It Ready: When doubt or fear strikes, be ready to raise that shield. Don't wait until you're under heavy fire to remember it's there!
- ➢ Polish It Up: Keep your faith strong through prayer, worship, and time with other believers.

Faith isn't just about believing; it's about acting on those beliefs, trusting that God is who He says He is and will do what He says He will do. Your Shield of Faith is what enables you to stand firm in the face of life's battles, confident that no matter what comes your way, God is there, protecting and guiding you.

Helmet of Salvation

Next, let's move on to the **Helmet of Salvation**. Think of it like the helmet you'd wear in a contact sport—it protects your head, your mind, and ultimately, your decision-making. Our spiritual enemy knows that if he can get into our heads, he can lead us astray. That's why we need the Helmet of Salvation.

Paul tells us in 1 Thessalonians 5:8, "But since we belong to the day, let us be sober, putting on faith and love as a breastplate, and the hope of salvation as a helmet." The helmet is about protecting our minds with the hope and assurance of salvation.

Again, back around 2008, doubt seemed to creep into every thought. I was questioning my purpose, my direction, and even my faith. It felt like I was under a constant barrage of negative thoughts. That's when I learned the importance of wearing my Helmet of Salvation—by reminding myself daily that my salvation is secure in Christ, and nothing can separate me from His love.

Charles Spurgeon once said, "Hope itself is like a star—not to be seen in the sunshine of prosperity, and only to be discovered in the night of adversity." The helmet represents that hope. It's our defense against the lies and doubts that try to penetrate our minds.

How to Wear the Helmet of Salvation Daily

- Remind Yourself of God's Promises: Write down key scriptures that affirm your salvation and review them regularly.
- Guard Your Mind: Be mindful of what you allow into your thoughts, filter out negativity and focus on what's true.
- Practice Gratitude: Reflect on your salvation and give thanks to God daily. Gratitude is a powerful shield against negative thinking.

When you wear the Helmet of Salvation, you protect your thoughts and your focus, ensuring that your mind stays aligned with God's truth and purpose.

Sword of the Spirit

Finally, let's talk about the **Sword of the Spirit**, which Paul tells us in Ephesians 6:17 is the "word of God." Unlike the other pieces of armor, the sword is both a defensive and offensive weapon. It's our tool for standing firm against the enemy's attacks, but also for advancing forward.

Jesus Himself demonstrated the power of the Sword of the Spirit when He was tempted by Satan in the wilderness. Each time Satan tried to tempt Him, Jesus countered with, "It is written," followed by scripture. He used the Word of God to cut down every lie and temptation thrown His way.

A few years ago, I faced a tough season of fear and anxiety. It was like every day was a battle in my mind. But I began to memorize and declare scriptures, like Psalm 23:4: "Even though I walk through the darkest valley, I will fear no evil, for you are with me; your rod and your staff, they comfort me." Speaking these truths out loud helped me stand firm and overcome the fear that was trying to paralyze me.

How to Use the Sword of the Spirit Daily

> ➢ Read and Study the Bible Regularly: The more you know God's Word, the sharper your sword becomes.
> ➢ Memorize Key Scriptures: Keep them in your heart and mind to use in times of need.
> ➢ Speak the Word Aloud: Declare God's promises out loud over your life and circumstances.
> ➢ Apply It: Don't just read the Word—live it out in your actions and decisions.

The Sword of the Spirit is your ultimate weapon in spiritual battles. It's powerful, precise, and effective. When you wield it, you're not just defending yourself; you're advancing the Kingdom of God.

As we conclude this first chapter, I hope you see that the **Armor of God** is more than just a metaphor—it's a practical guide for living a life of faith and preparedness. Each piece of armor is designed to protect us, not only from the physical challenges we might face but also from the spiritual battles that come our way.

Whether it's the **Belt of Truth** that keeps us grounded in honesty, the **Breastplate of Righteousness** that guards our hearts, the **Shoes of Peace** that give us steady footing, the **Shield of Faith** that defends against fear and doubt, the **Helmet of Salvation** that protects our minds, or the **Sword of the Spirit** that helps us fight back against the lies of the enemy—each piece is essential to our readiness.

In the pages ahead, we'll dive deeper into what it means to live a life fully equipped with this armor. We'll explore practical ways to integrate faith with preparedness, balancing the spiritual and physical aspects of readiness. Remember, the most important preparation you can make is spiritual. When your heart, mind, and spirit are fortified, you'll be ready for whatever comes your way.

So, are you ready to continue this journey? Let's move forward with confidence, knowing that with God's armor, we are prepared to face any challenge.

Onward, warrior. The adventure is just beginning.

Prayer for the Armor of God

Lord, clothe me in Your armor. Help me to wear the Belt of Truth, the Shield of Faith, and the Helmet of Salvation with courage. Strengthen my heart with Your righteousness, and let me wield the Sword of Your Word to stand firm in every trial.

In Jesus' name, Amen.

Chapter 2
Preparing Spiritually and Physically

When it comes to preparedness, most people think about storing food, gathering supplies, and learning survival skills. And those are important. But as we explored in Chapter 1, preparedness goes deeper than that—it's also about being spiritually ready for whatever life throws our way.

In this chapter, we'll explore how spiritual and physical preparedness go hand in hand. Being prepared spiritually strengthens your resilience, builds inner peace, and provides a strong foundation when challenges arise. And when you combine that with practical physical preparation, you create a holistic approach that equips you to face any situation with confidence.

Balancing Spiritual and Physical Preparedness

Think of spiritual preparedness as the root system of a tree. It's hidden beneath the surface, but it's what gives the tree stability, nourishment, and strength. Physical preparedness is like the branches and leaves, visible to everyone and critical for the tree's survival and growth. When both are strong, the tree can weather any storm.

Why Spiritual Readiness Matters

Builds Resilience

Spiritual readiness helps you stay calm and centered, even in crisis. Philippians 4:13 reminds us, "I can do all things through Christ who strengthens me." When you know where your true strength comes from, you're less likely to be shaken by fear or uncertainty.

Provides Inner Peace

Jesus said, "Peace I leave with you; my peace I give you" (John 14:27). Spiritual preparation gives you a peace that goes beyond understanding—a peace that remains, even when the world feels chaotic.

Guides Decision-Making

When you're spiritually grounded, you're better equipped to make wise, discerning decisions, even under pressure.

Proverbs 3:5-6 encourages us: "Trust in the Lord with all your heart and lean not on your own understanding; in all your ways submit to him, and he will make your paths straight."

Why Physical Readiness Matters

Ensures Practical Safety

Having the right supplies, skills, and plans in place ensures that you and your family are safe and secure in emergencies.

Reduces Stress

Being physically prepared means you're not scrambling in a crisis. You've already taken steps to anticipate needs, which reduces stress and anxiety.

Empowers You to Help Others

When you're prepared, you're in a better position to assist others who may not be. As Galatians 6:2 says, "Carry each other's burdens, and in this way, you will fulfill the law of Christ."

Integrating Spiritual and Physical Preparedness

So how do we integrate these two forms of preparedness? Here are some practical steps that have worked for me:

Start Your Day with Prayer and Planning

Begin each day by grounding yourself spiritually—through prayer, meditation, and scripture reading. Then, spend a few minutes reviewing your emergency plans or checking your supplies. It's a great way to keep both your spiritual and physical readiness top of mind.

Create a 'Preparedness Journal'

Keep a journal where you note both your spiritual reflections and your practical preparedness plans. Write down scriptures that encourage you, along with a checklist of supplies you need or skills you want to learn.

Practice 'Faith-Driven Drills'

Combine regular emergency drills (like fire drills, first aid practice, etc.) with spiritual practices. Pray together as a family during these drills, asking for wisdom, peace, and protection.

Connect with a Community

Join or form a group of like-minded individuals who share your values and preparedness goals. Encourage each other spiritually and physically, share resources, and support one another.

When Faith and Preparedness Worked Together

Let me share how spiritual and physical preparedness came together during the 2020 pandemic. When the lockdowns were announced, I was fortunate to have some physical preparations in place. My pantry was stocked with non-perishables, I had a supply of essentials, and I'd even set aside some extra cleaning and hygiene products. These practical steps definitely eased some of the initial stress and uncertainty.

However, as the days turned into weeks and then months, I realized that physical preparation alone wasn't enough. The isolation, fear, and constant barrage of troubling news took a toll on my mental and spiritual well-being. I recognized the critical importance of spiritual preparation and that I needed to prioritize it in our families' lives.

During the chaos, we took moments to pray together. We connected virtually with our church community, finding strength in our shared experiences and mutual support. These spiritual practices provided a sense of peace and purpose that no amount of stored goods could offer. They helped us maintain hope and resilience in the face of unprecedented challenges.

This experience taught me that true preparedness involves both the practical and the spiritual. While my physical preparations kept me comfortable, it was my spiritual foundation that truly sustained us through the uncertainty and helped me extend support to others in need. It reminded me of the verse from Isaiah 41:10: "Do not fear, for I am with you; do not be dismayed, for I am your God." Those times reinforced for me that spiritual and physical readiness are not separate but intertwined—they support each other and make us stronger.

Reflection Points

> - **What areas of your life need more spiritual or physical preparedness?**
>
> - **How can you integrate these two forms of readiness in your daily routine?**
>
> - **Who in your community could benefit from your preparedness knowledge or support?**

As you move forward, remember that true preparedness goes beyond what you can see or touch. It's about aligning your heart, mind, and body to be ready for whatever comes your way. By combining spiritual and physical preparation, you're building a foundation that is strong, resilient, and ready to withstand any storm.

In the next chapter, we'll dive deeper into the practical side of preparedness, exploring essential skills and strategies that every believer should know. Let's continue this journey of faith and readiness together.

Stay grounded, stay ready, and let's keep moving forward.

Prayer for Preparing Spiritually and Physically

Father, guide me as I seek to balance my spiritual and physical preparedness. May my heart be rooted in Your peace, and my hands ready for action. Help me trust in Your provision while also taking steps to protect and provide for my loved ones.

In Jesus' name, Amen.

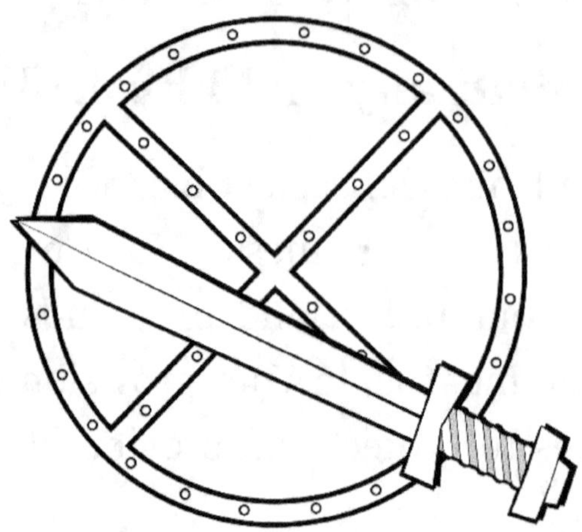

Chapter 3
Essential Skills for Every Believer

Being prepared isn't just about having the right gear—it's also about developing the right skills. Whether it's knowing how to start a fire in the wilderness or understanding how to pray in times of crisis, these skills are essential for every believer who wants to be ready for whatever life throws their way.

Think about it: when the storms of life hit—and they will—it's not just the physical tools that'll keep you afloat. It's the mental fortitude, the spiritual resilience, and the practical know-how that'll make the difference between merely surviving and truly thriving.

This chapter is about equipping you with a toolkit of *some* practical and spiritual skills that will get you started and help you navigate both the seen and unseen challenges. These aren't just skills for survival; they're skills for thriving, for growing stronger in your faith, and for becoming a source of strength to those around you.

Imagine standing firm in your faith when everything seems to be crumbling. Picture yourself being the calm in the storm, the light in the darkness for your family and community. That's what we're aiming for here.

But here's the thing—these skills aren't just for "someday." They're for right now, for everyday life. Because let's face it, we're all in a spiritual wilderness sometimes. And the more prepared you are, the more confidently you can walk through whatever valley you find yourself in.

So, buckle up. This journey isn't just about survival techniques—it's about becoming the person God has called you to be, no matter what comes your way. It's about being ready not just to weather the storm, but to dance in the rain. Are you ready? Let's dive in and continue to build that toolkit of faith and preparedness.

Spiritual Skill:

Developing a Strong Prayer Life

Prayer is more than just a spiritual discipline; it's a lifeline. It connects us to God, gives us strength, and provides clarity in times of confusion. James 5:16 says, "The prayer of a righteous person is powerful and effective." A strong prayer life equips us to face any challenge with confidence.

How to Build This Skill

- ➢ *Create a Prayer Routine*
  - o Set aside a specific time each day for prayer. Start with just five minutes if you're new to this.
- ➢ *Use Scripture in Your Prayers*
  - o Pray God's promises back to Him. This not only strengthens your faith but aligns your desires with His will.
- ➢ *Pray with Others*
  - o Join a prayer group or partner with a friend. Praying with others encourages you and helps build a habit.

I remember a particularly difficult time when I was overwhelmed with anxiety about the future. My son was experiencing some health issues that would affect him for life. As a father I felt particularly helpless. Here is my child, suffering, and I cannot "fix it". I'm supposed to be "fix it Dad". It seemed like everything was uncertain, and I didn't know which direction to take. But I decided to dedicate time every morning to prayer, even when I didn't feel like it. Over time, I noticed a shift—clarity replaced confusion, and peace replaced panic. That experience showed me that prayer isn't just something we do; it's a skill we develop, a muscle we strengthen.

Physical Skill:

Basic First Aid

Being able to provide first aid in an emergency can make the difference between life and death. It's a practical skill that everyone should have. Proverbs 21:31 says, "The horse is made ready for the day of battle, but victory rests with the Lord." Being ready means taking practical steps, like knowing how to administer basic first aid.

How to Build This Skill

> *Take a First Aid Course*
>> o Enroll in a local class or online program. Learn CPR, wound care, and how to handle fractures.

> *Put Together a First Aid Kit*
>> o Assemble a basic kit for your home and car. Make sure you know how to use every item in it.

> *Practice Regularly*
>> o Refresh your skills periodically. Practice bandaging, CPR techniques, and other essential tasks with family or friends.

A few years ago, I was hiking with friends when one of them slipped and fell, spraining his or her ankle. Thankfully, I had taken a basic first aid course, and we were able to bandage the injury and create a makeshift splint using materials from our backpacks. That incident reminded me that having the right skills can turn a potentially serious situation into a manageable one.

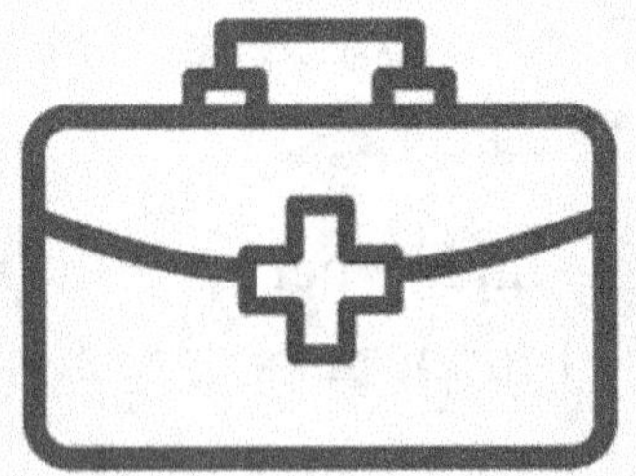

Spiritual Skill:

Studying Scripture

Understanding and applying God's Word is foundational to spiritual growth and preparedness. Psalm 119:105 says, "Your word is a lamp to my feet and a light to my path." When we study scripture, we're better equipped to discern God's will and find direction in uncertain times.

How to Build This Skill

- ➢ *Set a Regular Time for Study*
    - o Dedicate specific times each week to delve into God's Word.
- ➢ *Use Study Tools*
    - o Utilize resources like commentaries, study Bibles, and online tools to deepen your understanding.
- ➢ *Journal Your Reflections*
    - o Write down what you're learning and how it applies to your life. This helps internalize God's teachings.

There have been many periods in my life of great uncertainty where I found myself feeling lost and without direction. Each time that I decide to commit to a Bible study plan, like say – diving deep into the book of Proverbs – I find that each verse provides comfort and guidance, and over time, I begin to feel grounded and more confident in God's plan. That experience helps in reinforcing in me the value of consistent, intentional study of scripture. If you are starting out, Proverbs makes it easy to read daily because it has 31 chapters, 1 chapter a day.

Physical Skill:

Navigational Techniques

Knowing how to navigate without modern technology is crucial in emergencies. It's easy to rely on GPS, but what if your phone dies, or you're in an area without service? Being able to read a map and use a compass can be lifesaving. Psalm 32:8 says, "I will instruct you and teach you in the way you should go; I will counsel you with my loving eye on you." Just as God guides us spiritually, we should be prepared to guide ourselves physically.

How to Build This Skill

> - *Learn to Read Maps and Use a Compass*
>   - Take a course or find tutorials online to learn these basics.
> - *Practice in a Familiar Area*
>   - Try using a map and compass on local trails or in a park to practice your skills.
> - *Join a Group*
>   - Consider joining a local hiking or orienteering group to gain practical experience.

Let me share an experience that truly taught me the value of navigation skills. I once participated in a team-building adventure that challenged us to hike to the summit of Mt. Whitney. This wasn't your average hike - it was a grueling 10-day journey with only basic necessities.

At the start, we were given just a map and a compass. Our instructions were simple yet daunting: reach specific daily checkpoints and ultimately, the summit. Then we were left to our own devices to make it happen.

Those 10 days were incredibly challenging. We had to rely on our map-reading skills and compass use to navigate the terrain. There was no GPS, no smartphones to fall back on - just our wits and these basic tools. We learned to read the landscape, to use natural landmarks to confirm our position, and to trust our calculations.

The journey tested not just our physical endurance, but our ability to work as a team and make critical decisions. Each day brought new challenges - steep inclines, unpredictable weather, and the constant pressure of reaching our checkpoints on time.

Despite the difficulties, we persevered. The sense of accomplishment when we finally reached the summit was indescribable. We had not only conquered the mountain but also mastered essential navigation skills that would serve us well beyond this adventure.

This experience drove home the importance of knowing how to navigate without relying on technology. It taught me that with the right skills and determination, we can overcome seemingly insurmountable challenges. More importantly, it showed me how crucial these basic navigation skills can be in unpredictable situations.

Reflection Points

- **Which skills do you feel confident in, and which could use some improvement?**

- **How can you integrate spiritual and physical skills into your daily routine?**

- **Who can you share these skills with, and how might they benefit?**

As you consider these essential skills, remember that preparedness is about more than just what you have—it's about what you know and how you grow. Each skill you develop makes you more capable, more confident, and more ready to face life's challenges.

In the next chapter, we'll explore the importance of community and how building strong connections can enhance both your spiritual and physical preparedness. Let's keep building together, one step at a time.

You're becoming stronger every day—spiritually and physically. Keep going.

Prayer for Essential Skills
for Every Believer

Lord, equip me with the skills I need to serve You and others. Strengthen my spirit through prayer and Your Word, and help me gain wisdom in practical matters. May I be a light to those around me, ready to respond with love and readiness.

In Jesus' name, Amen.

Helping Others on Their Faith & Preparedness Journey

Your Review Can Make a Difference

"Whoever brings blessing will be enriched, and one who waters will himself be watered." – Proverbs 11:25

Those who share their wisdom and encouragement strengthen not just themselves but also others. Let's build a stronger, faith-filled community together!

Would you help someone like you—someone who desires to be spiritually and practically prepared for life's uncertainties?

My mission with *Spiritual Survival* is to equip believers with both the knowledge of the Armor of God and real-world readiness. But to reach more people, I need your help.

Most people choose books based on reviews. By leaving your thoughts on Amazon, you could help a fellow believer find the guidance they've been looking for.

It costs nothing and takes less than a minute, but it could change someone's faith and preparedness journey.

Your review could help...

- ...one more person stand firm in faith.
- ...one more family feel prepared for uncertain times.
- ...one more believer discover the power of the Armor of God.
- ...one more household gain peace of mind.

✓ ...one more life be strengthened in both faith and action.

To leave a review and help others on their journey, scan the QR code or visit the link below:

📖 **https://www.amazon.com/review/review-your-purchases/?asin=B0DJZSTR7D**

If you believe in helping others, you're my kind of person. Thank you from the bottom of my heart!

- A Prayerful Prepper
P. Thompson

Chapter 4
Building a Strong Community

No one is meant to face life's challenges alone. Whether it's a personal crisis, a natural disaster, or a moment of spiritual doubt, having a strong community around you can make all the difference. In this chapter, we'll explore why community is essential for both spiritual and physical preparedness and how you can build and strengthen your connections.

Imagine for a moment: The power's out, the stores are empty, and uncertainty hangs in the air like a thick fog. Now picture the same scenario, but this time, you're surrounded by neighbors who have your back, fellow believers who lift you up in prayer, and friends who share their resources without hesitation. That's the power of community, and it's not just a nice-to-have—it's a must-have for anyone serious about being prepared for whatever life throws their way.

But here's the thing: Strong communities don't just happen. They're built, nurtured, and maintained through intentional effort and God's grace. It's about more than just knowing your neighbors' names or showing up to church on Sundays. It's about forging deep, meaningful connections that can withstand the storms of life—both literal and figurative.

Remember, being prepared isn't just about stockpiling supplies or learning survival skills (though those are important). It's about cultivating a network of relationships that can provide emotional support, spiritual guidance, and practical help when you need it most. And equally important, it's about positioning yourself to be that support for others.

As we embark on this exploration of community, I challenge you to open your heart and mind. Some of what we discuss may push you out of your comfort zone. That's okay—growth rarely happens within the confines of what's comfortable. But I promise you this: the rewards of building a strong, Christ-centered community are worth every ounce of effort you put in.

So, are you ready to transform your approach to preparedness? Are you willing to invest in relationships that could quite literally save your life one day? Let's dive in and discover how to build a community that not only weathers the storms but emerges stronger because of them.

The Spiritual Importance of Community

The Bible is filled with examples of how God designed us for community. In Hebrews 10:24-25, we're encouraged to "consider how we may spur one another on toward love and good deeds, not giving up meeting together, as some are in the habit of doing, but encouraging one another." Community is not just a nice-to-have; it's a vital part of our spiritual journey.

Why Community Matters Spiritually

Encouragement in Faith

Being surrounded by fellow believers helps us stay strong in our faith. Proverbs 27:17 says, "As iron sharpens iron, so one person sharpens another." We help each other grow, learn, and remain steadfast.

Accountability

A good community holds us accountable. When we are tempted to stray or lose focus, our friends and mentors can help keep us on the right path.

Shared Wisdom

We all have different experiences and insights. By sharing with others, we gain a broader perspective and learn new ways to grow spiritually.

I remember a time when I was struggling with a major decision in my life. I felt lost and unsure of what to do. I turned to my small group at church, and they provided both the spiritual encouragement and practical advice I needed. Their support helped me find clarity and gave me the courage to move forward in faith. That experience taught me that community is like a safety net; it catches you when you fall.

The Practical Importance of Community

Beyond spiritual benefits, a strong community is invaluable in practical preparedness. Ecclesiastes 4:9-10 reminds us, "Two are better than one... if either of them falls down, one can help the other up." In times of crisis, whether it's a natural disaster or a personal emergency, having a network of people you can rely on is crucial.

Why Community Matters Practically

Shared Resources

In an emergency, you might need supplies, skills, or information that others in your community can provide.

Physical Support

When disasters strike, communities come together to support one another with shelter, food, and other necessities.

Emotional Strength

Simply knowing you're not alone can make a huge difference in how you cope with stress and fear during a crisis.

During a particularly severe winter storm, our community came together in an incredible way. Neighbors helped each other clear driveways, shared supplies, and checked in on elderly residents. The sense of solidarity and mutual support was powerful. It was a reminder that, in times of need, a strong community is worth more than any amount of individual preparation.

Building and Strengthening Your Community

So, how do you build and maintain a strong community? Here are some practical steps:

Get Involved Locally

Join local groups, whether it's a church, a neighborhood association, or a hobby club. The more you're involved, the more connections you'll make.

Offer Help Before It's Needed

Be proactive in reaching out to others. Small acts of kindness, like helping a neighbor with yard work or offering a meal to someone in need, build trust and relationships.

Host Gatherings

Organize regular gatherings with friends, family, or neighbors. These don't have to be formal—just a chance to connect, share, and build bonds.

Communicate Openly and Honestly

Be open about your needs and encourage others to do the same. Vulnerability fosters deeper relationships and mutual support.

Pray for Each Other

Make it a habit to pray for those in your community and let them know you're doing so. Prayer strengthens bonds and brings God's presence into your relationships.

Reflection Points

- **Who are the people in your life you can count on in a crisis? How can you strengthen those relationships?**

- **What steps can you take to build a stronger community around you?**

- **How can you use your skills, resources, or time to serve others in your community?**

Remember, community is not just something we build in times of need—it's something we nurture every day. By investing in relationships, offering help before it's asked, and being willing to receive support, you create a network that can withstand any storm.

In the next chapter, we'll dive into the importance of maintaining a positive mindset and how it can impact your spiritual and physical preparedness. Together, we'll continue to build a life that's ready for anything.

Keep reaching out, keep building, and keep growing. Your community needs you, and you need them.

Prayer for Building a Strong Community

God of unity, thank You for the gift of community. Help me build strong connections with others, rooted in love and support. Teach me how to serve and encourage my neighbors as we face challenges together. May our community be a reflection of Your Kingdom on earth.

In Jesus' name, Amen.

Chapter 5
Maintaining a Positive Mindset

In the face of adversity, our greatest ally is often our own mind. Whether confronted with natural disasters, personal crises, or spiritual challenges, the power of a positive outlook can be transformative. This chapter explores how nurturing a hopeful perspective and developing mental resilience are not just beneficial, but essential components of both spiritual and physical preparedness.

Imagine standing at the foot of a mountain, gear in hand, ready to climb. The journey ahead is daunting, but your mindset will determine whether you see an insurmountable obstacle or an exhilarating challenge. Similarly, in life's trials, a positive mindset can be the difference between feeling defeated and finding the strength to persevere.

As Proverbs 23:7 reminds us, "For as he thinks in his heart, so is he." Our thoughts shape our reality, influencing how we perceive and respond to the world around us. In other words, the way we think determines how we live. A positive mindset allows us to see opportunities instead of obstacles, find hope in difficult situations, and maintain peace amid chaos. By cultivating a positive mindset, we equip ourselves with a powerful tool for navigating life's uncertainties and emerging stronger on the other side.

Key Reasons a Positive Mindset is Crucial

Builds Resilience

> A positive outlook helps us bounce back from setbacks. It encourages us to keep going, even when the road gets tough. Romans 12:12 reminds us to "Be joyful in hope, patient in affliction, faithful in prayer."

Enhances Problem-Solving

> When we're optimistic, we're more likely to think creatively and find solutions to problems. Philippians 4:8 encourages us to focus on what is true, noble, right, pure, lovely, and admirable.

Strengthens Faith

> Maintaining a positive mindset is an act of faith. It shows trust in God's goodness, even when we don't see the whole picture. Hebrews 11:1 tells us, "Now faith is confidence in what we hope for and assurance about what we do not see."

There have been plenty of times in my life where I faced a significant personal challenge. It would feel like everything was falling apart, and I couldn't see a way forward. We have all been in those moments. We have all felt that despair. But instead of giving in to that despair, I tried to choose to focus on the things I was grateful for and kept reminding myself of God's promises. I am not perfect at it; I still often catch myself and bring my mindset back around. Over time, my circumstances didn't change overnight, but my perspective sure would—and that made all the difference. I began to see God's hand at work in ways I hadn't noticed before. Mindset is a choice, and choosing hope makes you stronger.

Overcoming Negative Thought Patterns

While cultivating a positive mindset is crucial, it's equally important to recognize and address negative thought patterns that can undermine our efforts. We all face negative thoughts from time to time, but learning to identify and reframe them is a powerful skill in maintaining emotional and spiritual resilience.

You may recognize some of these common negative thought patterns.

All-or-Nothing Thinking

> Seeing things in black and white categories.

Overgeneralization

> Viewing a single negative event as a never-ending pattern of defeat.

Mental Filter

> Dwelling on a single negative detail and ignoring positive aspects.

Jumping to Conclusions

> Making negative interpretations without supporting facts.

Practice Thought Awareness: Keep a thought journal for a week. Write down negative thoughts as they occur, noting the situation that triggered them. This practice can help you identify patterns and recurring themes in your thinking.

Challenge the negative thoughts. When you catch yourself in a negative thought pattern, ask:

Is this thought based on facts or feelings?

Am I jumping to conclusions?

What would I say to a friend who had this thought?

Reframe/Replace negative thoughts with more balanced, realistic ones.

For example, instead of "I can't handle this," try "This is challenging, but I've overcome difficulties before."

Replace "Everything is going wrong" with "Some things are difficult right now, but other areas of my life are going well."

Use Scripture to Combat Negativity. Memorize verses that counteract common negative thoughts.

Here are a few you can memorize today!

For anxiety

"Do not be anxious about anything, but in every situation, by prayer and petition, with thanksgiving, present your requests to God." (Philippians 4:6)

For feeling overwhelmed

"I can do all this through him who gives me strength." (Philippians 4:13)

Practice Mindfulness

Stay present in the moment rather than dwelling on past mistakes or future worries. Mindfulness can help break the cycle of negative rumination.

Seek Support

Share your struggles with trusted friends, family, or a counselor. Sometimes, an outside perspective can help us see things more clearly and positively. Remember, overcoming negative thought patterns is a process that requires patience and practice. As 2 Corinthians 10:5 encourages us, we are to "take captive every thought to make it obedient to Christ." By consistently working to recognize and reframe negative thoughts, we strengthen our positive mindset and build greater resilience for whatever challenges may come.

Practical Steps to Cultivate a Positive Mindset

So, how can we maintain a positive mindset, even when times are tough? Here are some practical steps that have worked for me:

Practice Gratitude Daily

Make it a habit to write down three things you're grateful for each day. This simple practice can shift your focus from what's wrong to what's right.

Speak Life

Pay attention to the words you use—both with others and yourself. Proverbs 18:21 reminds us that "the tongue has the power of life and death." Choose words that bring life, hope, and encouragement.

Stay Grounded in God's Word

Read and meditate on scriptures that build your faith. Consider verses like Isaiah 41:10: "Do not fear, for I am with you; do not be dismayed, for I am your God." Repeat these promises daily.

Surround Yourself with Positive People

Spend time with people who uplift and encourage you. Ecclesiastes 4:12 says, "Though one may be overpowered, two can defend themselves. A cord of three strands is not quickly broken."

Limit Negative Inputs

Be mindful of what you consume—whether it's news, social media, or entertainment. Focus on what uplifts and inspires you rather than what drags you down.

Find Purpose in Serving Others

Shift your focus outward by finding ways to serve and help others. Helping others not only blesses them but also brings joy and fulfillment to your own life.

Reflection Points

- **What thoughts or beliefs might be holding you back from having a positive mindset?**

- **How can you begin to practice gratitude, even in small ways?**

- **Who in your life inspires you to think positively, and how can you spend more time with them?**

Finding Strength Through Mindset

Let me share another example of how maintaining a positive mindset made a difference in my life. A few years ago, I was navigating a difficult financial season. I'm sure we've all been in this position. The bills were piling up, and the outlook seemed grim. I could have easily given in to fear, but I decided to focus on what I could control. I took steps to budget better, sought wise counsel, and trusted God to provide.

One day, out of the blue, I received an unexpected refund check that covered a significant portion of my bills. It reminded me of 2 Corinthians 9:8: "And God is able to bless you abundantly, so that in all things at all times, having all that you need, you will abound in every good work." That experience reinforced that maintaining hope and trusting in God's provision opens the door for unexpected blessings.

A positive mindset doesn't mean ignoring reality or pretending everything is fine when it isn't. Instead, it's about choosing to see things from God's perspective and trusting that He is always at work, even in the darkest times.

In the next chapter, we'll explore how to create a personalized preparedness plan that aligns with your values, needs, and faith journey. Together, we'll continue building a life that's ready for whatever comes next.

Keep your head up, your heart open, and your faith strong. The best is yet to come.

Prayer for Maintaining a Positive Mindset

Lord, guard my thoughts and guide my heart. Help me focus on Your promises and cultivate a mindset of hope and faith. When negativity creeps in, remind me that Your peace surpasses all understanding. Help me to be a source of encouragement to those who are weary.

In Jesus' name, Amen.

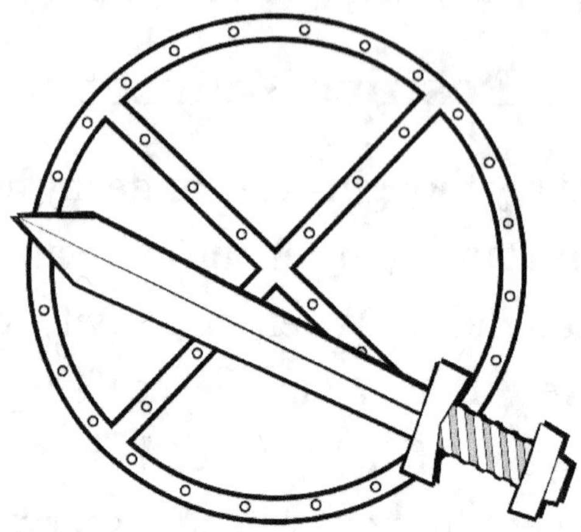

Chapter 6
Creating Your Personalized Preparedness Plan

In the journey of preparedness, one size does not fit all. Just as each person's walk with faith is unique, so too is their path to readiness. This chapter will guide you through crafting a preparedness plan that not only addresses your physical needs but also aligns with your spiritual values and personal circumstances.

Imagine your preparedness plan as a tapestry, woven with threads of faith, practical wisdom, and personal insight. Each strand represents a different aspect of your life - your family's needs, your spiritual growth, your physical resources, and the unique challenges you may face. By carefully intertwining these elements, you create a robust and flexible plan that can withstand life's uncertainties.

As we embark on this process, remember the words of Jeremiah 29:11: "For I know the plans I have for you," declares the Lord, "plans to prosper you and not to harm you, plans to give you hope and a future." Let this verse be our guiding light as we develop a plan that not only prepares us for earthly challenges but also deepens our trust in God's ultimate plan for our lives.

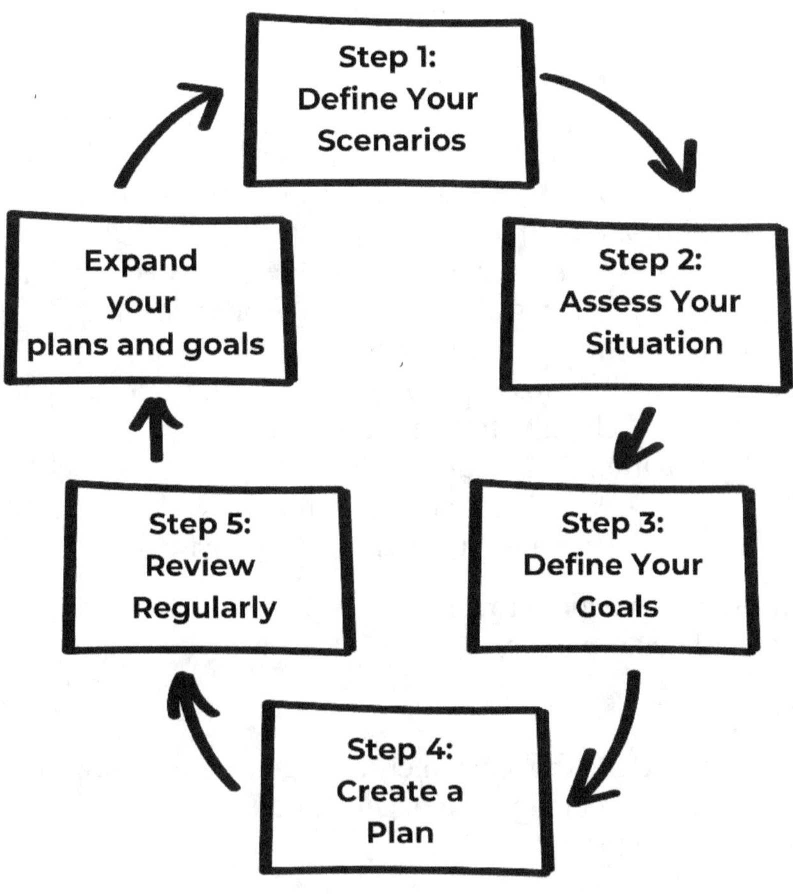

Step 1: Define Your Preparedness Scenarios

Before we dive into assessment and planning, it's essential to clearly define what we're preparing for. This step helps focus our efforts and ensures our plan addresses specific, relevant challenges.

Consider the following categories of potential scenarios. These are just some thought-provoking topics. Each of us has different life circumstances. You can add more depending on your particular situation or environment.

- *Natural Disasters*
  - o Depending on your location, this could include hurricanes, earthquakes, floods, wildfires, or severe winter storms.
- *Man-made Emergencies*
  - o These might include extended power outages, civil unrest, or economic crises.
- *Personal or Family Crises*
  - o Job loss, major illness, or unexpected life changes fall into this category.
- *Spiritual Challenges*
  - o Periods of doubt, spiritual warfare, or tests of faith are important to prepare for as well.

Here are some ideas to help you define your scenarios you will build your plan for.

Research

> Look into the most likely emergencies for your area. Local emergency management offices often provide this information.

Reflect

> Consider your personal circumstances. What challenges are you most likely to face?

Pray

> Ask for God's guidance in identifying areas where you need to be prepared. James 1:5 tells us, "If any of you lacks wisdom, you should ask God, who gives generously to all without finding fault, and it will be given to you."

Prioritize

> You can't prepare for everything at once. List your scenarios in order of likelihood and potential impact.

Discuss

> Talk with your family about these scenarios. Their input can provide valuable perspectives you might have overlooked.

Remember, the goal isn't to fear these potential challenges, but to be wisely prepared. As Proverbs 22:3 says, "The prudent see danger and take refuge, but the simple keep going and pay the penalty."

When I first started defining the scenarios we needed to prepare for, I had a bit of an eye-opening moment. I realized that while I had some supplies stored at home, I had completely overlooked our vehicles. Both my wife and I commute to work daily, spending a significant amount of time on the road. It hit me that our cars were a major point of vulnerability I hadn't planned for at all.

This realization led me to create comprehensive vehicle emergency kits for each of our cars. I included items like a first aid kit, blankets, non-perishable snacks, water, a flashlight with extra batteries, basic tools, and a portable phone charger. I also made sure to add season-specific items like ice scrapers for winter and extra coolant for summer.

This experience taught me the importance of thinking through our daily routines and identifying potential risks in all aspects of our lives, not just at home. It also reminded me that preparedness isn't a one-time event but an ongoing process of evaluation and adaptation. Now, I feel much more confident knowing that whether we're at home or on the road, we have supplies to help us handle unexpected situations.

Step 2: Assess Your Current Situation

The first step in creating a personalized preparedness plan is to assess where you are right now. Ask yourself these questions.

What are your immediate needs?

> Consider your family size, health conditions, location, and potential risks (e.g., natural disasters, economic downturns).

What resources do you currently have?

> Take stock of your existing supplies, skills, and community connections.

What are your spiritual strengths and areas for growth?

> Reflect on your current spiritual practices, such as prayer, scripture study, and community involvement.

Proverbs 27:12 repeats what we hear in 22:3, "The prudent see danger and take refuge, but the simple keep going and pay the penalty." Assessing your situation is about being prudent—understanding your risks and preparing accordingly.

Step 3: Define Your Priorities and Goals

Next, define what matters most to you. What are your top priorities in terms of preparedness?

Spiritual Goals

> Consider how you want to grow spiritually through this process. Is it deepening your prayer life, studying scripture more, or building stronger connections with your community?

Physical Goals

> Identify the key areas of physical preparedness you need to focus on. This could include building a food storage supply, learning first aid, or improving your physical fitness.

Family Goals

> Discuss with your family what preparedness looks like for you as a unit. Align your goals to ensure everyone is on the same page.

Initially, my top priority was ensuring that my family had enough food and water to last through a potential emergency. I started to build up for 3 days, then 3 weeks, and moved on to 3 months. It is not a once and done process but a continuous process. While building up my stockpiles I prayed and reflected, I realized that I also needed to prioritize my spiritual growth. I made it a goal to not only build up my physical supplies but also to deepen my relationship with God through daily devotions.

Step 4: Create a Step-by-Step Plan

With your priorities and goals in mind, create a step-by-step plan. Break down each goal into manageable actions.

- *Spiritual Steps*
    - Set aside time daily for prayer and scripture study.
    - Join a small group or community to support your spiritual growth.
    - Start a prayer journal to track your progress and reflect on what God is teaching you.
- *Physical Steps*
    - Begin building your emergency supply kit with essential items like water, non-perishable food, first aid, and tools.
    - Take a class on basic survival skills, such as CPR or fire safety or get your HAM Radio license.
    - Establish emergency communication plans with your family.
- *Family Steps*
    - Involve your family in the planning process. Assign specific roles and responsibilities.
    - Practice emergency drills together regularly.
    - Discuss and agree on a meeting place in case of evacuation.

Luke 14:28 says, "Suppose one of you wants to build a tower. Won't you first sit down and estimate the cost to see if you have enough money to complete it?" This verse reminds us of the importance of planning and preparation before taking action.

Step 5: Review and Adjust Regularly

A preparedness plan isn't a one-time effort; it's an ongoing process. Regularly review your plan and make adjustments as needed.

Evaluate Your Progress

> Set aside time each month or quarter to review your plan. What's working well? What needs improvement?

Make Adjustments

> As your circumstances change, be willing to adapt your plan. Maybe your family has grown, or you've moved to a new area with different risks. Stay flexible.

Stay Spiritually Attuned

> Continue to seek God's guidance and wisdom in your planning. Proverbs 16:9 reminds us, "In their hearts humans plan their course, but the Lord establishes their steps."

I learned the importance of regular review the hard way. After developing a thorough plan, I felt pretty confident—until we moved to a new area prone to different kinds of natural disasters. I realized that my plan needed some serious adjustments. That experience taught me the value of staying flexible and continually seeking God's direction.

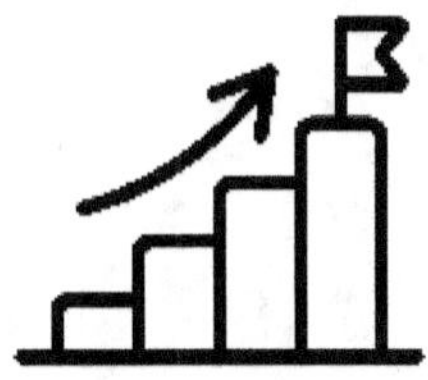

Reflection Points

- **What are your top priorities for preparedness? How do they align with your spiritual values?**

- **What specific steps can you take this week to start building your personalized preparedness plan?**

- **How can you involve your family or community in the planning process?**

Creating a personalized preparedness plan is about more than just checking off items on a list. It's about aligning your efforts with your faith, your values, and your unique circumstances. Remember, this is a journey—a process of growth, learning, and trust in God's provision.

In the next chapter, we'll explore how to stay spiritually strong and physically prepared during long-term challenges. Let's keep building, growing, and trusting together.

You're well on your way to being ready for whatever comes next. Keep planning, keep praying, and keep pressing forward.

Prayer for My Preparedness Plan

Father, grant me wisdom as I prepare for the unknown. Help me make decisions that honor You and provide for my family's needs. Let my plans be a reflection of trust in You, knowing that ultimately, You are our refuge and strength.

In Jesus' name, Amen.

Chapter 7
Staying Spiritually Strong and Physically Prepared During Long-Term Challenges

Life's journey often includes seasons of extended trials—periods where our faith, resilience, and preparedness are tested not just for days or weeks, but for months or even years. Whether facing a prolonged economic downturn, battling a chronic illness, or weathering a spiritual drought, these long-term challenges demand a unique blend of unwavering faith and sustained readiness.

In this chapter, we'll explore how to cultivate a spirit of endurance that honors God and keeps us prepared, no matter how long the storm may last. As the prophet Isaiah reminds us, "Those who hope in the Lord will renew their strength. They will soar on wings like eagles; they will run and not grow weary, they will walk and not be faint" (Isaiah 40:31). Let this promise be our anchor as we learn to stay spiritually strong and physically prepared for the long haul.

Why Resilience Matters in Long-Term Challenges

Resilience is the ability to endure, adapt, and keep moving forward, even when the path is difficult. James 1:2-4 reminds us, "Consider it pure joy, my brothers and sisters, whenever you face trials of many kinds, because you know that the testing of your faith produces perseverance. Let perseverance finish its work so that you may be mature and complete, not lacking anything."

Key Reasons Resilience is Essential

Keeps You Grounded in Faith

> Resilience helps you maintain your trust in God, even when you can't see the end of the trial. It's about believing in His promises and holding on to hope.

Enables You to Adapt

> Long-term challenges often require flexibility. Resilience allows you to adapt your plans and mindset as circumstances change.

> Builds Inner Strength: Each time you persevere through a difficulty, you become stronger and more capable of handling future challenges.

I once weathered a season of relentless challenges that tested every aspect of my life. It began with the sudden loss of my job, which quickly spiraled into financial turmoil. As if that weren't enough, health issues cropped up, adding physical discomfort to my growing list of worries. These compounding problems began to chip away at my faith, leaving me grappling with spiritual doubts.

Night after sleepless night, I lay awake, my mind racing with anxiety and despair. Exhaustion became my constant companion, both physically and emotionally. Yet, in the depths of this overwhelming period, I made a crucial decision: instead of succumbing to hopelessness, I would focus on small, daily victories.

I started with simple acts of faith—dedicating a few minutes each day to prayer, taking short walks to clear my mind, or finding solace in the Psalms. But perhaps the most unexpected source of comfort came from an unlikely place: dental floss.

You see, I'd never been diligent about flossing, typically cramming in a few weeks of halfhearted effort just before my annual dentist visit. But during this trying time, I decided to make daily flossing a personal challenge. It may sound trivial, but it became something I could control amidst the chaos—a small, tangible accomplishment each day.

Tracking my prayers and my flossing side by side might seem an odd pairing, but these small, consistent acts became anchors in my stormy sea of uncertainty. Over time, these seemingly insignificant habits of faith and self-care began to accumulate. To my surprise, I found myself growing stronger and more resilient, even as external circumstances remained challenging.

This experience taught me the power of perseverance through small, daily commitments. It showed me that even in our darkest hours, we can find ways to move forward, one tiny step—or floss—at a time.

Practical Strategies for Staying Spiritually Strong

Daily Spiritual Practices

Keep your spiritual disciplines consistent, even when life is hard. Set aside time each day for prayer, scripture reading, and worship. Even a few minutes can make a big difference.

Memorize and Meditate on Scripture

Find verses that speak to your situation and memorize them. Meditate on them throughout the day. Scriptures like Psalm 46:1— "God is our refuge and strength, an ever-present help in trouble"—can provide comfort and strength.

Stay Connected with a Faith Community

Don't isolate yourself. Stay connected with your church, small group, or other faith communities. They can provide encouragement, support, and accountability.

Use Worship as a Weapon

Worship isn't just for Sundays; it's a powerful tool for spiritual strength. Sing praises, listen to worship music, or even dance before the Lord like David did. Worship changes our focus from our problems to God's power.

Cultivating Spiritual Resilience for Long-Term Challenges

Expanding on the strategies for staying spiritually strong, this section focuses on deeper practices that will help you maintain spiritual resilience during prolonged trials.

Embracing Lament

When prayers seem unanswered, express your pain to God as seen in the Psalms of lament. Try writing your own psalm, sharing your honest emotions while affirming your trust in God.

Practicing Gratitude in Adversity

Train yourself to notice even the smallest blessings during hardships. Keep a gratitude journal, noting even tiny mercies each day. As 1 Thessalonians 5:18 advises, "Give thanks in all circumstances."

Reframing Unanswered Prayers

Instead of viewing unanswered prayers as neglect, consider them as opportunities for deeper trust. Reflect on Romans 8:28: "And we know that in all things God works for the good of those who love him."

Cultivating Stillness

Learn to be still before God and allow His presence to renew you. Psalm 46:10 reminds us, "Be still, and know that I am God."

Finding God in the Ordinary

Practice noticing God's presence in your everyday tasks, transforming the mundane into spiritual connection.

Deepening Scriptural Engagement

Study characters in the Bible who endured long trials—like Job and Joseph—and learn from their perseverance.

Adapting Spiritual Disciplines

Modify your spiritual practices to fit your current season. If sitting in prayer is hard, try prayer walks. If reading long passages feels overwhelming, meditate on shorter scriptures.

Embracing Community in New Ways

When gathering is difficult, seek creative ways to maintain connection—online prayer groups, virtual Bible studies, or handwritten letters.

Serving Others

Look for opportunities to serve others during your struggles. Helping others brings perspective and purpose to your own trials.

Celebrating Small Victories

Recognize and celebrate each moment of spiritual growth. Every decision to choose faith over doubt is a victory.

Nurturing Mental Well-being in Long-Term Challenges

While we often focus on spiritual and physical preparedness, maintaining mental health is equally crucial during extended periods of difficulty. Long-term challenges can take a significant toll on our mental well-being, potentially leading to anxiety, depression, or burnout if not addressed.

Recognize the Importance of Mental Health

Acknowledge that caring for your mental health is not a luxury, but a necessity. It's a vital part of your overall well-being and ability to persevere. Proverbs 17:22 reminds us, "A cheerful heart is good medicine, but a crushed spirit dries up the bones."

Seek Professional Help

There's no shame in reaching out to mental health professionals. Counselors, therapists, or pastoral counselors can provide valuable tools and perspectives to help you navigate your challenges. Just as you'd see a doctor for a physical ailment, seek help for your mental health when needed.

Practice Mindfulness and Meditation

Incorporating mindfulness techniques can help manage stress and anxiety. Try simple breathing exercises or guided meditations. These practices can be aligned with your faith – consider meditating on scripture or practicing contemplative prayer.

Maintain Healthy Relationships

Strong, positive relationships are crucial for mental health. Stay connected with supportive friends and family. Be honest about your struggles and allow others to help. Ecclesiastes 4:9-10 tells us, "Two are better than one... If either of them falls down, one can help the other up."

Establish Routines

Creating and maintaining daily routines can provide a sense of normalcy and control, even when other aspects of life feel chaotic.

Practice Self-Compassion

> Be kind to yourself. Recognize that it's okay to have difficult days and that healing and growth take time. Treat yourself with the same compassion you'd offer a friend facing similar challenges.

Engage in Physical Activity

> Regular exercise is not just good for your body; it's beneficial for your mind too. Even a short daily walk can help boost mood and reduce stress.

Limit Negative Inputs

> Be mindful of how news, social media, or certain relationships might be affecting your mental state. It's okay to set boundaries to protect your peace of mind.

Remember, taking care of your mental health is not selfish or unspiritual. It's an essential part of stewarding the life God has given you and equipping yourself to face long-term challenges with resilience and hope.

Practical Strategies for Staying Physically Prepared

Maintain Physical Health

> Take care of your body with regular exercise, a balanced diet, and adequate rest. 1 Corinthians 6:19-20 reminds us, "Do you not know that your bodies are temples of the Holy Spirit... Therefore honor God with your bodies."

Keep Your Supplies Stocked

Regularly check your emergency supplies and rotate food, water, and other items to keep them fresh. Make a habit of replenishing supplies as they are used.

Practice Skills Regularly

Stay sharp by practicing essential skills like first aid, cooking with limited resources, and other preparedness techniques.

Plan for the Long-Term

Consider long-term needs like gardening, water purification, or alternative energy sources. Being prepared for extended situations can provide peace of mind.

Long-Term Resilience Plan Template

Identify Your Challenges.

List the long-term challenges you're facing.

Spiritual Resilience

Daily spiritual practice

Weekly spiritual goal

Scripture for meditation

Prayer focus

Mental Well-being

Self-care activities

Professional support needed

Mental Well-being (continued)

Stress-relief techniques

Physical Preparedness

Health goals

Emergency supplies to maintain

Skills to practice/learn

Relationship Support

Key support people

Community involvement

Personal Growth

New skill to learn

Suggested reading

Personal Growth (continued)

Goal to work towards

Gratitude and Joy

Daily gratitude practice

Activities that bring joy

Adaptive Strategies

If [challenge] happens, I will

When I feel [emotion], I will

Progress Tracking

Weekly review day

Monthly milestone

Inspirational Quote/Verse:

Remember to review and adjust your plan regularly as circumstances change and you grow.

Reflection Points

- **What are the greatest challenges you're currently facing, and how can you cultivate resilience in these areas?**

- **How can you maintain both spiritual and physical preparedness during prolonged difficulties?**

- **Who in your life can support you through long-term challenges, and how can you reach out to them?**

When Perseverance Pays Off

I once knew a family who faced a series of devastating natural disasters that impacted their home and livelihood. Over several years, they endured floods, storms, and economic hardships. But they remained steadfast in their faith and commitment to preparedness. They prayed together daily, kept their community close, and supported each other through each challenge. Slowly but surely, they rebuilt their lives, and their faith grew stronger through every storm. Their story reminds me of Romans 5:3-4: "Not only so, but we also glory in our sufferings, because we know that suffering produces perseverance; perseverance, character; and character, hope."

Long-term challenges test our strength, patience, and faith in ways we may never expect. But remember, with God's help, you have everything you need to persevere. Stay spiritually rooted, remain physically prepared, and lean on the support of your community.

In the next chapter, we'll explore how to find peace and purpose, even in the midst of chaos. We'll discover practical ways to live a life that is both prepared and purposeful, filled with faith and readiness.

Keep your eyes on God, your heart full of hope, and your spirit strong. You're not just surviving— you're growing.

Prayer to Stay Spiritually Strong and Physically Prepared During Long-Term Challenges

God, in times of long-lasting trials, give me the strength to persevere. Help me remain rooted in faith, and may my resilience be a testimony of Your sustaining power. Keep me spiritually strong and physically prepared for whatever comes.

In Jesus' name, Amen.

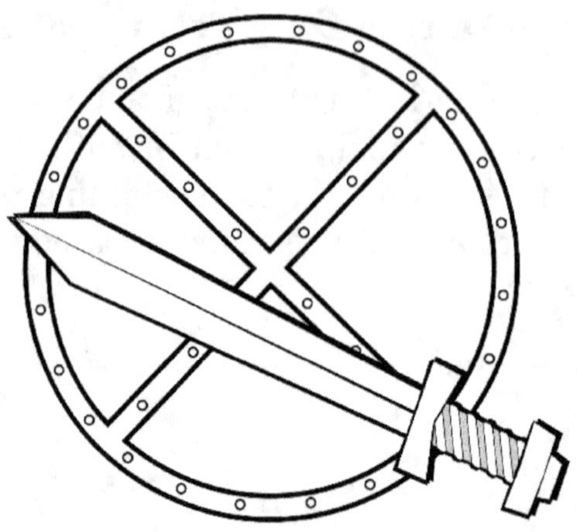

Chapter 8
Finding Peace and Purpose in Preparedness

In the storm of uncertainty, where does one find an anchor? As we've explored in the previous chapter, long-term challenges can test our resilience to its limits. Yet, amidst the turbulence of life's unpredictability, there exists a profound opportunity - not just to survive, but to thrive. This chapter invites you on a journey beyond mere readiness, into the realm where preparedness meets purpose, and where chaos gives way to an unshakeable peace.

Imagine a life where your efforts to be prepared aren't driven by fear but fueled by faith. A life where each action you take isn't just a checkbox on a survival list, but a deliberate step towards fulfilling God's calling. This is the intersection of peace and purpose in preparedness - a place where readiness becomes a form of worship, and where trust in God's providence transforms anxiety into assurance.

As we delve into this crucial aspect of our preparedness journey, we'll discover how aligning our efforts with our faith can lead to a deeper sense of peace and a clearer understanding of our purpose. We'll explore practical ways to cultivate this peace, even in the face of uncertainty, and how to infuse every aspect of our preparedness with divine purpose.

Are you ready to transform your approach to preparedness? Let's embark on this transformative journey together, guided by the wisdom of Scripture and the peace that surpasses all understanding.

Why Peace Matters in Preparedness

True peace comes from knowing that, no matter what happens, God is in control. Jesus said in John 14:27, "Peace I leave with you; my peace I give you. I do not give to you as the world gives. Do not let your hearts be troubled and do not be afraid." This peace is different from the temporary calm the world offers—it's a deep, abiding peace that remains steady, even in the midst of chaos.

Key Reasons Peace is Essential:

Provides Clarity in Decision-Making: When we are at peace, we think more clearly and make wiser decisions. It's hard to plan effectively when we're anxious or fearful.

> *Reduces Stress and Anxiety*

A peaceful heart and mind are less affected by stress and worry. Philippians 4:6-7 encourages us, "Do not be anxious about anything, but in every situation, by prayer and petition, with thanksgiving, present your requests to God. And the peace of God, which transcends all understanding, will guard your hearts and your minds in Christ Jesus."

> ➢ *Deepens Trust in God*

> Peace comes from trusting that God is good and that His plans for us are always for our ultimate good, even when we don't understand them. Romans 8:28 reminds us, "And we know that in all things God works for the good of those who love him, who have been called according to his purpose."

I recall a time when my life felt like it was spinning out of control. Everything I had planned seemed to be unraveling, and anxiety began to take over. But in the middle of that storm, I chose to focus on God's promises of peace. I began to pray and meditate on scriptures like Isaiah 26:3: "You will keep in perfect peace those whose minds are steadfast, because they trust in you." Slowly, my heart calmed, and I felt a peace that transcended the chaos around me. That experience taught me that true peace doesn't depend on our circumstances but on our relationship with God.

Why Purpose Matters in Preparedness

Purpose gives our efforts meaning. When we know why we are doing something, it gives us motivation and direction. 1 Corinthians 10:31 reminds us, "So whether you eat or drink or whatever you do, do it all for the glory of God." Preparedness with purpose isn't just about surviving; it's about thriving, living intentionally, and fulfilling God's call on our lives.

Key Reasons Purpose is Essential

➤ Keeps You Focused

A clear sense of purpose keeps you focused on what truly matters, even when distractions or difficulties arise.

➤ Encourages Perseverance

Knowing your "why" gives you the strength to keep going, even when it's hard. Galatians 6:9 encourages us, "Let us not become weary in doing good, for at the proper time we will reap a harvest if we do not give up."

➤ Aligns Your Actions with Your Faith

When our preparedness efforts are aligned with God's purposes, they become acts of worship. They are a way of loving others, stewarding our resources, and trusting in God's provision.

During one particularly challenging season, I struggled with the purpose of all my preparedness efforts. It seemed like a lot of work for something that might never happen. But then I realized that my preparedness wasn't just about me—it was about being ready to help others, to be a light in dark times, and to steward the resources God had given me wisely. That realization gave me renewed energy and joy in the process. It wasn't just about storing food or water; it was about living a life aligned with God's heart and purposes.

Discovering Your Unique Purpose in Preparedness

As believers, we understand that God has a unique plan for each of us. Jeremiah 29:11 reminds us, "For I know the plans I have for you," declares the Lord, "plans to prosper you and not to harm you, plans to give you hope and a future." This promise extends to every aspect of our lives, including our preparedness efforts.

Your purpose in preparedness goes beyond simply stockpiling supplies or learning survival skills. It's about aligning your efforts with God's calling for your life and using your unique gifts to serve others and glorify Him, even in times of crisis.

Consider these aspects as you reflect on your unique purpose:

Your Spiritual Gifts

> How can your spiritual gifts be applied to preparedness? For example, if you have the gift of teaching, you might be called to educate others about preparedness from a biblical perspective.

Your Life Experiences

> How have your past experiences, including hardships, equipped you to help others in times of need?

Your Passions

> What aspects of preparedness are you most passionate about? This could be a clue to your unique calling.

Your Community's Needs

What specific needs exist in your community that you feel called to address through your preparedness efforts?

Your Skills and Talents

How can your professional skills or personal talents contribute to preparedness efforts in a unique way?

Reflection Exercises

Scripture Meditation

Spend time meditating on Romans 12:4-8.

> *For as we have many members in one body, but all the members do not have the same function, so we, being many, are one body in Christ, and individually members of one another. Having then gifts differing according to the grace that is given to us, let us use them: if prophecy, let us prophesy in proportion to our faith; or ministry, let us use it in our ministering; he who teaches, in teaching; he who exhorts, in exhortation; he who gives, with liberality; he who leads, with diligence; he who shows mercy, with cheerfulness.*

How might this passage apply to your role in preparedness within the body of Christ?

Gift Inventory

List your top three spiritual gifts, skills, or talents. For each, write down how it could be used in a preparedness context to serve others.

Vision Journaling

Imagine it's five years from now, and you've fully embraced your purpose in preparedness. Write a detailed description of what that looks like. How are you serving others? What impact are you making?

Community Needs Assessment

Conduct a simple survey in your church or community about preparedness needs. Reflect on how your unique abilities might address these needs.

Prayer for Guidance

Spend dedicated time in prayer, asking God to reveal His purpose for you in preparedness. Keep a journal of any insights or direction you receive.

Remember, discovering your purpose is often a journey rather than a sudden revelation. Be patient with yourself and remain open to God's guidance. As you align your preparedness efforts with His will, you'll find a deeper sense of peace and fulfillment in your journey.

Practical Steps to Find Peace and Purpose in Preparedness

Start with Prayer

Ask God to show you His purpose for your preparedness journey. Pray for peace and clarity as you make plans.

Reflect on Your Motivations

Take time to consider why you are preparing. Are your efforts driven by fear, or are they rooted in trust and purpose?

Align Your Actions with Your Values

Ensure that your preparedness efforts reflect your faith and values. Let love, generosity, and trust in God guide your actions.

Serve Others

Find ways to use your preparedness to bless others. Whether it's sharing supplies, offering your skills, or providing support, preparedness becomes meaningful when it serves a higher purpose.

Stay Grounded in Scripture

Keep your focus on God's Word. Verses like Jeremiah 29:11—"For I know the plans I have for you," declares the Lord, "plans to prosper you and not to harm you, plans to give you hope and a future"—remind us of God's good intentions for us.

Reflection Points

- **What does peace mean to you, and how can you cultivate it in your daily life?**

- **What is your "why" for being prepared? How does it align with God's purposes for you?**

- **How can you use your preparedness to serve others and bring glory to God?**

Finding peace and purpose in preparedness isn't about having all the answers or never facing fear. It's about choosing to trust God's plan, even when it's unclear, and finding joy in living intentionally. As you continue your preparedness journey, remember that God is with you every step of the way, guiding, providing, and giving peace that surpasses all understanding.

In the final chapter, we'll wrap up our journey together, reflecting on what we've learned and how to move forward with confidence and faith.

Keep trusting, keep preparing, and keep finding peace and purpose in all you do. Your journey is just beginning.

A Prayer for Peace and Purpose

Heavenly Father,

In the middle of all this uncertainty and chaos, I come to You, the Prince of Peace. Your Word promises in Philippians 4:7 that Your peace, which transcends all understanding, will guard my heart and mind in Christ Jesus. I claim that promise now.

Lord, when I feel overwhelmed by the challenges before me, help me remember Isaiah 26:3, which says, "You will keep in perfect peace those whose minds are steadfast, because they trust in You." Steady my mind on Your unchanging love and faithfulness.

God of all comfort, as I prepare for whatever may come, guide my steps. Help me to trust in You with all my heart and lean not on my own understanding, as Proverbs 3:5-6 instructs. Direct my path and show me the purpose You have for me in this season.

When I'm tempted to worry about tomorrow, remind me of Your words in Matthew 6:33-34, to seek first Your kingdom and Your righteousness. Grant me the peace that comes from knowing You will provide for all my needs.

Father, like David, I pray in Psalm 139:23-24, "Search me, God, and know my heart; test me and know my anxious thoughts. See if there is any offensive way in me and lead me in the way everlasting." Reveal to me any areas where I'm not fully trusting You, and help me surrender them.

Lord Jesus, You said in John 14:27, "Peace I leave with you; my peace I give you. I do not give to you as the world gives. Do not let your hearts be troubled and do not be afraid." I receive Your peace now. Let it fill me, calm me, and empower me to face whatever lies ahead.

Holy Spirit, guide me in using the gifts and resources You've given me to serve others and glorify You, even in times of crisis. Help me to be a beacon of Your peace to those around me.

I thank You, Lord, that even as I pray, You are working all things together for good, as promised in Romans 8:28. In times of doubt, strengthen my faith. In times of fear, be my courage. In times of confusion, be my wisdom.

I rest in Your love, trusting that You are with me always, to the very end of the age (Matthew 28:20).

In Jesus' name, Amen.

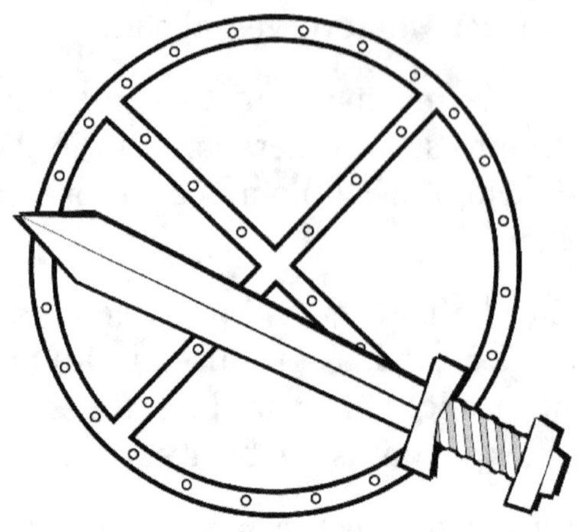

Chapter 9
Moving Forward with Faith and Readiness

As we stand at the threshold of a new beginning, let us pause and reflect on the transformative journey we've undertaken together. From donning the Armor of God to finding peace amidst chaos, we've explored the multifaceted landscape of faith-based preparedness. But make no mistake—this is not the end. Rather, it's the dawn of a new chapter in your life, one where faith and readiness intertwine to create a tapestry of purpose, resilience, and hope.

Imagine for a moment the person you were when you first opened this book. Now, consider who you've become— armed with knowledge, fortified by faith, and equipped with practical skills. You stand ready, not just to face life's challenges, but to thrive in the midst of them. As Ephesians 6:13 reminds us, "Therefore put on the full armor of God, so that when the day of evil comes, you may be able to stand your ground, and after you have done everything, to stand."

In this final chapter, we'll not only recap the essential lessons we've learned but also chart a course for the road ahead. We'll explore how to integrate these principles into your daily life, ensuring that your journey of faith and preparedness continues long after you've turned the last page of this book.

Are you ready to step into this new chapter of your life with confidence, faith, and purpose? Let's embark on this final leg of our journey together, knowing that it's just the beginning of a lifetime of growth, readiness, and unwavering trust in God's plan.

Recap of Key Themes

Throughout this book, we've emphasized that true preparedness is about more than stockpiling supplies or learning survival skills—it's about aligning your heart, mind, and actions with God's purposes. It's about:

Putting on the Armor of God

Recognizing that spiritual readiness is the foundation for all other forms of preparedness.

Balancing Spiritual and Physical Preparedness

Understanding that both aspects are essential for facing life's challenges with confidence and resilience.

Building Strong Communities

Knowing that no one is meant to face life's trials alone and that community is a crucial part of preparedness.

Maintaining a Positive Mindset

Realizing that your mindset can either propel you forward or hold you back, and that a hopeful outlook is a powerful tool.

Finding Peace and Purpose in Preparedness

Discovering that when your efforts align with God's will, preparedness becomes a meaningful and fulfilling journey.

Taking Action

Moving Forward with Confidence

Now that you've learned these principles, how do you move forward?

Start Small and Stay Consistent

Begin with small, manageable steps and build from there. Consistency is more important than perfection. Remember, growth is a process.

Reflect Regularly

Take time to reflect on what you've learned and how you can apply it. Ask yourself, "What is one thing I can do today to be more prepared spiritually or physically?"

Stay Connected to God and Others

Keep your relationship with God at the center of your preparedness journey. Stay connected with your community and support each other as you grow together.

Embrace the Journey

Preparedness is not a destination but a journey. Enjoy the process, find joy in the small victories, and trust that God is with you every step of the way.

Looking back on my own journey, I realize that every step—no matter how small—has brought me closer to understanding what it means to live a life of faith and readiness. I've learned that it's not about having all the answers or being fully prepared for every situation. It's about trusting God, staying faithful, and taking one step at a time. My hope is that you find the same peace, purpose, and confidence in your own journey.

Overcoming Obstacles in Your Preparedness Journey

As you embark on this journey of faith-based preparedness, you may encounter challenges that test your resolve. Remember, obstacles are not roadblocks but opportunities for growth. Let's explore some common challenges and strategies to overcome them:

Feeling Overwhelmed

The task of becoming prepared can seem daunting, leading to paralysis or procrastination. Remember Matthew 6:34, "Therefore do not worry about tomorrow, for tomorrow will worry about itself. Each day has enough trouble of its own." Break your preparedness journey into small, manageable steps. Focus on one task or skill at a time, celebrating each accomplishment along the way. This approach will help you make steady progress without feeling overwhelmed by the big picture.

Financial Constraints

Limited resources can make it difficult to acquire supplies or invest in training. In these moments, trust in God's provision (Philippians 4:19) while being a good steward of your resources. Start with low-cost or free preparedness activities like skill-building, community networking, or repurposing items you already own. Gradually build your supplies over time, prioritizing essential items first. Remember, preparedness is more about knowledge and mindset than accumulating stuff.

Lack of Support from Family or Friends

Your loved ones may not understand or support your preparedness efforts. Approach the topic with patience and love, as 1 Corinthians 13:4 teaches.

Love suffers long and is kind; love does not envy; love does not parade itself, is not puffed up;

Share your motivations and the peace it brings you. Lead by example, showing how preparedness aligns with your faith and values. Pray for understanding and look for opportunities to gently involve them in your journey. Over time, your consistent and positive approach may help them see the value in what you're doing.

Maintaining Motivation

Initial enthusiasm may wane over time, especially during periods of relative stability. As Galatians 6:9 encourages, "Let us not become weary in doing good, for at the proper time we will reap a harvest if we do not give up." Set regular reminders to review and update your preparedness plans. Join or create a support group to stay accountable and encouraged. Regularly reflect on your 'why' – your purpose in being prepared. This will help you stay motivated even when the immediate need isn't apparent.

Balancing Preparedness with Daily Life

Finding time for preparedness activities amidst busy schedules and responsibilities can be challenging. Remember the wisdom of Ecclesiastes 3:1, "There is a time for everything, and a season for every activity under the heavens." Integrate preparedness into your daily routines – practice skills during family time, incorporate food storage into your meal planning, or listen to educational podcasts during your commute. By weaving preparedness into your everyday life, it becomes a natural part of who you are rather than an additional burden.

Fear and Anxiety

Focusing on potential disasters can lead to fear or anxiety. In these moments, ground yourself in God's promises. Isaiah 41:10 reminds us, "So do not fear, for I am with you; do not be dismayed, for I am your God." Use your preparedness activities as an opportunity to deepen your faith and trust in God. Practice gratitude for His current provisions and protection. Remember that your preparations are an act of stewardship and love, not a response to fear. Let your faith be stronger than your fears.

Information Overload

The vast amount of preparedness information available can be overwhelming and sometimes contradictory. In these moments, recall Proverbs 3:5, "Trust in the LORD with all your heart and lean not on your own understanding." Prayerfully discern which information aligns with your values and needs. Focus on reliable, reputable sources. Remember that preparedness is a journey – you don't need to know everything at once. Start with the basics and gradually expand your knowledge over time, always filtering information through the lens of your faith and practical wisdom.

Remember, every obstacle you overcome strengthens your resilience and deepens your faith. As James 1:2-4 encourages us, "Consider it pure joy, my brothers and sisters, whenever you face trials of many kinds, because you know that the testing of your faith produces perseverance. Let perseverance finish its work so that you may be mature and complete, not lacking anything."

When you face challenges in your preparedness journey, take a moment to pray, seek wisdom from God and trusted mentors, and remember why you started this journey. Your efforts, rooted in faith and wisdom, are building a foundation of readiness that will serve you and your loved ones well, come what may.

Final Reflection Points

- What are the top three lessons you've learned from this book, and how will you apply them?

- What steps will you take today to move forward with faith and readiness?

- Who in your life can you encourage or support on their preparedness journey?

Closing Thoughts

As we close this chapter, remember that true preparedness is not just about stockpiling supplies or mastering survival skills. It's about cultivating a heart that trusts in God's providence, a mind that's ready for action, and hands that are willing to serve. The journey you've embarked upon is more than mere survival—it's about thriving in God's purpose for your life, come what may.

Now is the time to put your faith into action. Take that first step today, whether it's creating an emergency kit, starting a prayer journal, or reaching out to build community. Remember, every journey begins with a single step, and God promises to guide your path (Proverbs 3:5-6). Don't wait for tomorrow; seize this moment to become the prepared, faithful steward God is calling you to be.

As you close this book, open your heart to the possibilities that lie ahead. You have been equipped, encouraged, and empowered. Now, go forth with confidence, knowing that the God who called you to prepare will be with you every step of the way. Your journey of faith-based preparedness starts now. Are you ready to answer the call?

"Have I not commanded you? Be strong and courageous. Do not be afraid; do not be discouraged, for the Lord your God will be with you wherever you go." - Joshua 1:9

Let this be your mantra as you continue your journey of preparedness.

Thank you for taking this journey with me. I am honored to have shared these thoughts, stories, and principles with you. May you find strength in the Lord, confidence in your preparations, and joy in every step of your path.

Keep moving forward with faith and readiness. You are prepared for whatever comes next.

Your Faith & Preparedness Journey Matters—Now Help Others on Theirs

Now that you have the tools to strengthen both your faith and your preparedness, it's time to pay it forward and help others find the same guidance.

Leaving an honest review of *Spiritual Survival* on Amazon will show fellow believers and preparedness-minded individuals where they can find the encouragement and practical wisdom they need to stand strong in uncertain times.

Your review is more than just words—it's a way to share hope, faith, and readiness with someone searching for the right path.

I truly appreciate your help. Faith-based preparedness grows stronger when we share our knowledge and experiences—and you're helping me do just that.

To leave a review and help others on their journey, scan the QR code or click the link below:

https://www.amazon.com/review/review-your-purchases/?asin=B0DJZSTR7D

If you love helping others, you're my kind of person. Thank you from the bottom of my heart!

- The Prayerful Prepper
P. Thompson

Ephesians 6:10-18 (NIV)

*Finally, be strong in the Lord and in his mighty power. Put on the full **armor of God**, so that you can take your stand against the devil's schemes. For our struggle is not against flesh and blood, but against the rulers, against the authorities, against the powers of this dark world and against the spiritual forces of evil in the heavenly realms. Therefore put on the full **armor of God**, so that when the day of evil comes, you may be able to stand your ground, and after you have done everything, to stand. Stand firm then, with the **belt of truth** buckled around your waist, with the **breastplate of righteousness** in place, and with your **feet fitted with** the readiness that comes from **the gospel of peace**. In addition to all this, take up the **shield of faith**, with which you can extinguish all the flaming arrows of the evil one. Take the **helmet of salvation** and the **sword of the Spirit**, which is the word of God. And pray in the Spirit on all occasions with all kinds of prayers and requests. With this in mind, be alert and always keep on praying for all the Lord's people.*

My Preparedness Action Plan

1. Spiritual Preparedness

My next step in strengthening my spiritual armor:

Scripture I will meditate on this month:

Spiritual discipline I will focus on developing:

---

2. Physical Preparedness

Skill I want to learn or improve:

Supplies I need to acquire or rotate:

Physical fitness goal:

---

3. Mental/Emotional Preparedness

Stress-management technique I will practice:

Positive habit I want to develop:

Book or resource I will study:

---

4. Family/Community Preparedness

Family emergency plan to create or review:

Community connection to strengthen:

Skill or resource I can share with others:

---

5. Financial Preparedness

Budget area to review or improve:

Savings goal:

Financial skill to learn:

---

6. Long-term Goals

3-month preparedness goal:

6-month preparedness goal:

1-year preparedness goal:

____

7. Reflection and Accountability

How will I track my progress?

____

Who will I share my goals with for accountability?

____

How often will I review and update this plan?

____

8. Prayer for My Preparedness Journey

____

____

____

Remember: "For God has not given us a spirit of fear, but of power and of love and of a sound mind." - 2 Timothy 1:7

Date:

____

Signature:

____

Commit your plans to the Lord, and He will establish your steps. (Proverbs 16:3)

Faith-Based Preparedness Checklist

Chapter 1

Introduction to Faith-Based Preparedness

☐ Reflect on the biblical basis for preparedness (e.g., Noah, Joseph)

☐ Identify your personal motivations for preparedness

☐ Pray for guidance in your preparedness journey

Chapter 2

Spiritual Preparedness - The Armor of God

☐ Study Ephesians 6:10-18 and understand each piece of spiritual armor

☐ Develop a daily prayer and Bible study routine

☐ Memorize key scriptures for encouragement during difficult times

Chapter 3

Physical Preparedness

☐ Create a basic emergency kit (food, water, first aid supplies)

☐ Learn and practice basic first aid skills

☐ Develop a family emergency plan

☐ Start a physical fitness routine to improve stamina and strength

Chapter 4

Mental and Emotional Preparedness

☐ Practice stress-management techniques (e.g., deep breathing, meditation on scripture)

☐ Build a support network of like-minded individuals

☐ Educate yourself on common psychological responses to emergencies

☐ Develop a positive, faith-based mindset for facing challenges

Chapter 5

Family and Community Preparedness

☐ Discuss preparedness with your family and assign roles

☐ Connect with neighbors and local community for mutual aid

☐ Identify and develop skills you can contribute to your community

☐ Participate in or organize a community preparedness event

Chapter 6

Financial Preparedness

☐ Create or review your household budget

☐ Build an emergency fund (aim for 3-6 months of expenses)

☐	Reduce debt and implement wise financial practices

☐	Consider long-term financial preparations (e.g., investments, insurance)

Chapter 7

Long-Term Challenges and Sustainability

☐	Learn basic food production skills (e.g., gardening, preserving)

☐	Develop a plan for long-term water and energy needs

☐	Acquire and learn to use manual tools for various tasks

☐	Study and practice sustainable living techniques

Chapter 8

Finding Peace and Purpose in Preparedness

☐	Reflect on your preparedness efforts and align them with your faith

☐	Identify ways to use your preparations to serve others

☐	Practice gratitude for God's provisions in your life

☐	Develop a personal mission statement for your preparedness journey

Chapter 9

Moving Forward with Faith and Readiness

☐ Review and update your preparedness plans regularly

☐ Set short-term and long-term preparedness goals

☐ Commit to continuous learning and skill development

☐ Share your knowledge and experiences with others

Spiritual Growth Checklist

☐ Daily prayer and scripture reading

☐ Regular church attendance and fellowship

☐ Participation in a Bible study or small group

☐ Practice of spiritual disciplines (e.g., fasting, serving)

☐ Sharing your faith with others

Remember: "Trust in the LORD with all your heart and lean not on your own understanding; in all your ways submit to him, and he will make your paths straight." - Proverbs 3:5-6

Use this checklist as a guide, adapting it to your personal circumstances and the leading of the Holy Spirit. Preparedness is a journey, not a destination. Take it one step at a time, always keeping your faith at the center of your efforts.

Resources for Continued Growth

Books

- The Holy Bible
- "American Red Cross First Aid : Responding to Emergencies" by American, Red Cross
- "The Complete Prepper's Survival Bible" by David Reynolds
- "Prepared: The 8 Secret Skills of an Ex-IDF Special Forces Operator That Will Keep You Safe" by Roy Shepherd
- "SAS Survival Handbook" by John 'Lofty' Wiseman
- "The Survival Medicine Handbook" by Joseph Alton and Amy Alton
- "The Encyclopedia of Country Living" by Carla Emery

Websites

- Ready.gov - Official website of the Department of Homeland Security
- **PrayerfulPrepper.com – Blending faith with readiness in today's unpredictable world.**
- SurvivalBlog.com - A popular preparedness and survival blog
- ModernSurvivalBlog.com - Practical preparedness information
- ThePrepperJournal.com - Articles on various preparedness topics

Online Communities

- r/preppers - Reddit community for preparedness discussions

- The Prepared Christian Forums - Faith-based preparedness community
- American Preppers Network - Large preparedness community with various topics

Courses and Training

- Red Cross First Aid and CPR Certification
- CERT (Community Emergency Response Team) Training
- Wilderness First Aid courses
- HAM Radio Prep (hamradioprep.com)
- Local extension office classes on food preservation and gardening
- Dave Ramsey's Financial Peace University

Podcasts

- "Prophecy Watchers" by Jonathan Cahn
- "The Survival Podcast" with Jack Spirko
- "In the Rabbit Hole Urban Survival"
- "Prepping 2.0" by The Prepared
- "Mind4Survival"

YouTube Channels

- Heart Dive with Kanoe Gibson & Holly Rigos
- Canadian Prepper
- City Prepping
- The Urban Prepper
- Corporals Corner

Remember to always filter the information you find through the lens of your faith and personal circumstances. Not all advice will be applicable to everyone, so use discernment and pray for guidance as you continue your preparedness journey.

Disclaimers

General Disclaimer: The information provided in this book is for educational and informational purposes only. It is not intended to replace professional advice or services. The author and publisher make no representations or warranties with respect to the accuracy or completeness of the contents of this work and specifically disclaim all warranties, including without limitation warranties of fitness for a particular purpose. Neither the author nor the publisher shall be liable for any damages arising from the use or misuse of the information provided.

Medical Disclaimer: This book may contain references to health, nutrition, and emergency preparedness practices. The information provided is not a substitute for professional medical advice, diagnosis, or treatment. Always seek the advice of your physician or other qualified health provider with any questions you may have regarding a medical condition or emergency preparedness plan.

Religious Disclaimer: This book reflects the personal beliefs and experiences of the author regarding faith and preparedness. The content is intended to inspire and inform, not to impose any specific religious doctrine. Readers are encouraged to consult with their spiritual advisors or religious leaders for guidance on matters of faith.

Legal Disclaimer: The author and publisher are not responsible for any loss, injury, or damage that may result from the use of the information contained in this book. Readers are advised to consider local laws and regulations before applying any of the practices or techniques discussed.